Aussie
Jokes & Riddles

JILL B. BRUCE
ILLUSTRATED BY **JAN WADE**

Kangaroo Press

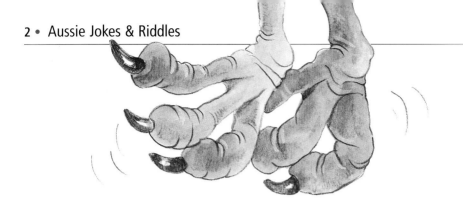

Little birdy up in the sky,
Dropped a message from on high.
As I wipe it from my eye,
I thank the Lord that emus don't fly.

What do you get if you cross a sheep with a kangaroo?

A woolly jumper.

What do koalas have that no other animal has?

Baby koalas.

What is a baby kookaburra after it is 10 days old?

Eleven days old.

How do you stop a Tasmanian devil from smelling?

Put a peg on its nose.

What do you get when a steamroller runs over a platypus?

A flatterpus.

Which side of a cassowary
has the most feathers?

The outside.

Can wallabies jump higher than a house?

Yes, houses can't jump.

What do you get if you cross a kangaroo with an elephant?

Great big holes all over Australia.

What is white on the outside, brown and warty
on the inside and hops?

A cane toad sandwich.

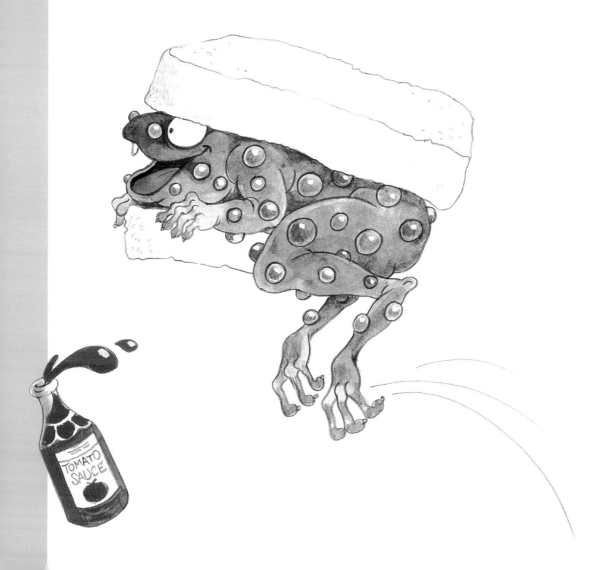

What do you get if you cross a dingo with a computer?

A dingo with lots of bytes

Where do Australian sheep shop?

At Wool-worth's because there are lots of baagains.

When do you put a frillnecked lizard in your brother's bed?

When you can't catch a crocodile.

What is the difference between
a wedgetailed eagle and ice cream?

Well if you don't know, I certainly won't send you for ice cream.

Why do white sheep eat more than black sheep?

Because there are more white sheep.

Which T.V. Show do Australian horses watch?

Neigh-bours.

Waiter, waiter! What is this bush fly doing in my soup?

Looks like the Australian crawl to me, sir.

How do echidnas kiss each other?

Very, very carefully.

Why did the bushranger take a bath?

He wanted to make a clean getaway.

What is a Kakadu crocodile's favourite game?

Snap!

What is smaller than bull ants pants?

A bush fly's tie.

Where do green tree
frogs leave their hats?

In the croakroom.

What is a kangaroo's favourite sport?

Long jump.

TOO FAR

VERY FAR

FAR

When do Wombats have eight feet?

When there are two of them.